2/97

INVENTORS & INVENTIONS

TELEPHONES

INVENTORS & INVENTIONS

TELEPHONES

GINI HOLLAND & AMY STONE

BENCHMARK BOOKS

MARSHALL CAVENDISH
NEW YORK

Benchmark Books
Marshall Cavendish Corporation
99 White Plains Road
Tarrytown, New York 10591-9001

Series created by The Creative Publishing Company

Library of Congress Cataloging-in-Publication Data

Holland, Gini.
 Telephones / Gini Holland & Amy Stone.
  p. cm. -- (Inventors & inventions)
 Includes index.
 Summary: Provides a history of the telephone and
telecommunications, including technical aspects and important
inventors.
 ISBN 0-7614-0065-6
 1. Telephone--Juvenile literature. 2. Telecommunication--Juvenile
literature. [1. Telephone. 2. Telecommunication.] I. Stone,
Amy, 1947- . II. Title. III. Series.
TK6165.H64 1995
621.385--dc20   95-17428
                 CIP
                 AC

Printed and bound in Hong Kong

Acknowledgments

Technical Consultant: Teodoro C. Robles, Ph.D.
Illustration on page 19 by Julian Baker

The publishers would like to thank the following for their permission to reproduce photographs:
AT&T (UK) Ltd., (32); B.T. Archives, (54); Alfred Y. Cho, (50, 51); Mary Evans Picture Library, (16, 26, 28, 31); Popperfoto, (46); Schomburg Center for Research in Black Culture, (20); Science & Society Picture Library, (8, 23, 30, 35, 39); Science Photo Library Ltd., (AT&T Bell Labs 36, 44, J-L Charmet 13, GE Astro Space 55, Hughes Aircraft Company 40, James King-Holmes 59, Library of Congress 11, Alfred Pasieka 48, Peter Ryan 52, Francoise Sauze 56); Tony Stone Images, (cover, frontispiece, 43, 57); UPI/Bettmann, (7, 10, 14, 18, 22, 24, 27, 37, 42).

(Cover and frontispiece) The telephone has now become an essential part of business and social life.

Contents

— Chapter 1 —
Improving Communications

Sarah glanced at the table with a critical eye. She was pleased to see that her birthday cake looked especially nice. When she heard a knock, Sarah ran to the door. The first of her friends had arrived, and within a few minutes, so had the last. When someone knocked again, Sarah let her mother answer. Even though the party had grown quite noisy, she could still hear her mother exclaim, "Oh my word, it's Uncle John. What a wonderful surprise! Sarah will be so pleased to see you. It's her birthday, you know."

"Of course, I know it's Sarah's birthday," John said. "That's why I'm here. Didn't you get my letter? I mailed it three weeks ago." "No, we didn't," Sarah's mother replied. "But the mail service from Colorado to Boston sometimes takes more than a month." Then Sarah's mother called to her son, "Henry, hitch up the carriage and go tell your father that his brother is here."

Sarah's birthday celebration took place in 1876, and communication was quite different from what it is today. Although he did write to say he was coming, Sarah's uncle failed to allow enough time for the letter to arrive. Cross-country letters were carried by stagecoach in the 1870s, and the trip took more than a month!

You may have noticed that Sarah's guests knocked at the door; they didn't ring an electric doorbell. Electricity was not yet used to power such things as doorbells or even lights in 1876. It wasn't used for telephones, either, which is why Sarah's brother had to use the carriage to go let his father know Uncle John had arrived.

This lithograph, The Progress of the Century *by Currier and Ives, was produced in 1876, the year the telephone was invented. It portrays some of the most important technical innovations of the nineteenth century. As well as the railroad and the steam engine in the background, it shows the telegraph — the forerunner of the telephone.*

Before the Telephone, the Telegraph

Local news moved slowly in the late 1800s, but national news traveled fast, thanks to the press. When Colorado became a state in 1876, the story appeared in the newspapers the next day. So did word of General George Custer's last stand against the Indians at Little Bighorn. National news was current because of the telegraph, a relatively recent invention.

Samuel F. B. Morse had invented the telegraph in 1837, and by 1861, telegraph lines had been built from one end of the country to the other. By 1866, a telegraph cable had been laid under the Atlantic Ocean.

Understanding the telegraph is a good basis for understanding how the telephone works because the telephone operates somewhat like a telegraph. In fact, the telephone grew out of attempts to make the telegraph send more than one sound at a time. The telegraph is only able to send long and short sounds over distance so it is far too simple to send the varying tones of the human voice.

How the Telegraph Works

An electric switch called a key or a transmitter sends a telegraphic message. Hooked by electrical wire to a battery, the key controls the flow of electricity from the battery through an electrical circuit. When the telegraph key is pushed down, the electricity starts flowing along an electric wire toward an electromagnet, a piece of soft iron with a wire wrapped around it. When electricity flows through the wire, it turns the iron into a magnet, or a force that can either pull or push something else made of metal or iron. The electromagnet in a telegraph system is attached to an iron bar called a receiver. When the electromagnet pulls the bar, the bar hits the electromagnet and makes a clicking sound. A sharp writing point is also attached to the bar, and as the bar moves up and down, the point makes marks on a piece of moving paper. Depending on how long the key is held down, the bar makes either a short or a long click, and the point makes either a dot or a dash. The clicking sounds or dots and dashes are part of the Morse code, which assigns combinations of dots and dashes to every letter of the alphabet.

The telegraph proved useful, but people had to rely on telegraph operators working in offices. In 1876, a telegram was reserved for special occasions and emergencies. The telephone, because it used everyday language instead of code and was simple enough for a child to master, quickly became the standard means of communication. Within twenty-five years of Sarah's birthday, a telephone would appear in almost every Boston home. But to most people in 1876, the idea that voices could move along an electrical wire sounded highly unlikely if not downright crazy.

A song cover shows a female telegraph operator. When the telephone came into use, women switchboard operators were found to be harder working than men and soon replaced them.

A Giant Mental Leap

The leap from telegraph to telephone was hard to make, even for scientists. Even though all of the materials and even the scientific principles were available and understood prior to its invention, the scientists who finally created the first telephone had to work at it for several years.

The man who invented the telephone became so famous that his name is known throughout the world: Alexander Graham Bell. Bell had been both a music and a speech teacher whose curiosity about sound and the human voice grew from his experience teaching people with hearing disabilities how to speak. Bell's understanding of how sound was received by the human ear, and therefore how it could be received by a mechanical device, came directly from his work with hearing-impaired people.

When Bell started experimenting, he didn't set out to invent a telephone. He simply wanted to improve the telegraph. During the early 1870s, Bell tried to invent an apparatus that could transmit several sounds at once over a single telegraph wire. He called it a harmonic telegraph. While performing experiments, Bell managed to send the sound of a vibrating steel reed over an electrical wire by attaching the reed to an electromagnet. In Bell's electrical circuit, both the transmitter and the receiver were reeds.

But Bell still hadn't figured out how to transmit more than one sound at a time. Then, he remembered something he had noticed during his earlier musical training — singing made the strings inside a piano, which vary in length and thickness, vibrate. Since reeds are essentially the same as strings, Bell reasoned that if he were to attach a variety of reeds of different thicknesses and lengths to an electromagnet, he would then be able to send varying tones over an electrical wire all at once. Bell knew he faced a practical problem. Transmitters and receivers made up of many different reeds would probably prove unmanageable. He needed something simpler, but what could it be? Bell's study of hearing gave him the missing clue.

AMAZING FACTS

The telegraph caught the public eye when it was used to catch a crook. After committing a murder, the criminal jumped on a train, figuring he couldn't be caught. He didn't know that his description as well as his seat number had been telegraphed ahead. When the culprit arrived at the next train station, the police nabbed him, and the story of his capture appeared in newspapers the next day. People were amazed that information could travel faster than trains.

Alexander Graham Bell (1847–1922)

Alexander Graham Bell was so talented he could have pursued a number of careers. As a boy, he played musical instruments perfectly without looking at notes, so his parents made sure he was given a musical education. But as much as he loved music, Bell loved what his father did even more. Bell's father had been a speech teacher, and Bell decided to become one, too.

Bell and his brothers were fascinated by the way speech was produced. As boys, they even made a model of a human skull and fitted it with a vocal device that made sounds with the help of a bellows. They made their skull wail "Ma-ma," and it sounded so much like a baby that neighbors came out to look for a crying child.

When he was sixteen, Bell tried out his teaching talents on the family pet by teaching his dog to "speak" actual English words with his help. He trained the Skye terrier to growl steadily while he moved the dog's mouth and vocal cords. The dog was able to say "How are you, grandmother?" but the dog's animal accent was quite

Alexander Graham Bell speaks into his new invention in 1876.

strong: The words actually sounded more like "Ow ah oo, ga-ma-ma."

In 1860, Bell became a full-time speech and music teacher, but he still managed to squeeze in room for another job — teaching people with hearing disabilities how to speak. Bell's mother had lost her hearing when Bell was a boy, and Bell had made up his mind to help others with the same disability.

Bell had been born in Scotland, but in 1870, his family moved to Canada, where his father hoped the climate would protect Bell against the tuberculosis that had killed Bell's two brothers. Bell moved from Canada to Boston in 1871, where he spent his days teaching and his late, late nights tinkering away in his attic studio.

Although Bell had no formal training in electricity, a combination of other talents and abilities helped him succeed as the inventor of the telephone. He had a sensitive ear and understood how speech was made. He was also very curious and could reason well. Bell wanted to know how things worked, and once he knew, he moved on to the next step: figuring out how to make them work even better. Bell was also ambitious. In the late 1800s, most Americans not only believed in the virtue of hard work, they believed that hard work could lead the way to wealth. Bell thought so, too.

Even though his financial backers told him to concentrate on an invention that would improve the telegraph, Bell pursued what he thought was a more interesting goal: sending the human voice across an electrical wire. Besides being ambitious, Bell was stubborn, a trait that helped him stick to what proved to be an invaluable task. On March 7, 1876, Bell was awarded a patent for the telephone, the most lucrative patent ever awarded in U.S. history.

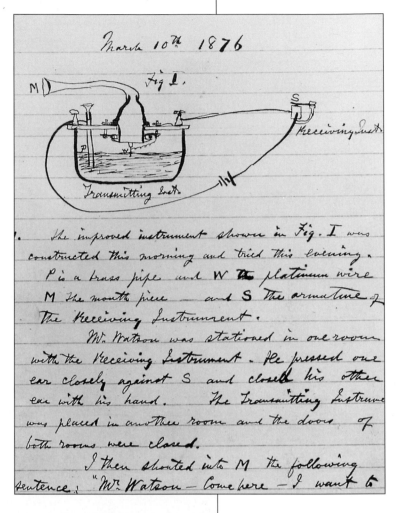

A page from Bell's notebook dated March 10, 1876, describes his first successful experiment.

The Diaphragm, a Perfect Transmitter

To learn more about patterns made by sound waves, Bell had been working with a device called a phonautograph that he had been using in his work with the deaf. He wanted to use it to give hearing-impaired people a visual model of human speech. When words were spoken, the vibrating membrane in the phonautograph moved a lever that scratched a wave pattern onto smoked glass, making a visual record of the spoken word.

Dissatisfied with how it worked, he replaced the steel membrane in the phonautograph with a human ear specimen he had obtained from a Boston ear specialist. With the entire ear in place, Bell marveled at the tiny eardrum's ability to move the relatively large bones of the inner ear. Recognizing this eardrum, a tiny membrane, as a diaphragm that was able to gather and transmit all the complex sounds of a human voice, Bell realized that a steel diaphragm did the same thing and could take the place of the reeds in his harmonic telegraph. A diaphragm was the transmitter and receiver he had been looking for. And, more importantly, Bell eventually realized that the vibrating diaphragm could reproduce the full range of sound waves produced by the human voice. In other words, Bell had figured out how a telephone might work.

Because he lacked mechanical ability, Bell hired an excellent electrical mechanic named Thomas A. Watson as his assistant. The duo worked together closely and successfully for several years.

Bell Applies for a Patent

Bell had at last put together all the ideas he need to develop a telephone, so on February 14, 1876, he applied for a patent, which he was quite anxious to receive. A patent owner has the exclusive rights to produce, sell, and make profits from the patented invention for a certain number of years. The government could award a patent to an inventor if no one else had

AMAZING FACTS

Bell's idea for the telephone began with a mistake! After reading a book in 1866 by the German inventor Hermann von Helmholz, Bell got the impression that Helmholz had been able to send vowel sounds produced by tuning forks over electrical wire. (Bell's understanding of German and electricity was quite limited at the time!) The inventor had not been able to do such a thing, which Bell soon realized. Still, the mistake started Bell thinking about the possibility of sending sound over electrical wire, and his thoughts eventually gave rise to the telephone.

been granted one for the same or a very similar invention.

Of course, the patent wouldn't make Bell rich unless he made a telephone that worked. Bell had to make a diaphragm that would transmit and receive the human voice. In less than a month, that's exactly what he did.

By attaching a wire to the diaphragm and putting the wire in water mixed with sulfuric acid, Bell believed he would have a transmitter that could send the alternating currents of the human voice. (Alternating current varies in intensity from instant to instant.) Bell had added acid to the liquid to increase its ability to conduct electricity. As the diaphragm vibrated, the wire moved up and down in the liquid. When the wire went down, its resistance — its ability to conduct electricity — lessened; when the wire went up, the resistance increased. In this way, the current through the wire and the liquid changed as the sound waves of the voice required. Bell had applied the important variable-resistance principle to make a transmitter that could send the human voice.

On March 10, 1876, Bell and Watson were ready to give the liquid transmitter its first try. Watson was at the receiving end of the wire, three rooms down from Bell. At the transmitting end, Bell had spilled some acid on his clothes and said, "Mr. Watson, come here, I want you!" Watson heard Bell's words quite clearly because they had, in fact, been transmitted over the electrical wire. The diaphragm and liquid transmitter had worked, and the first phone call — a plea for help — had been made.

This prototype telephone was constructed by Alexander Graham Bell in 1875. It consists of a coil of wire, a magnetic arm, and a taut membrane. Sound causes the membrane to vibrate. This moves the magnetic arm, and the magnet induces a fluctuating electric current in the coil. The electrical signal is reconverted into sound by identical equipment at the other end of the circuit.

Elisha Gray (1835–1901)

When the time is right for an invention — when known scientific principles can lead the way to a discovery that people need — it's not uncommon for more than one scientist to be working toward the same goal. And if the goal promises fame and fortune, it's likely that the inventors will race against each other to see who can reach the end of the scientific trail first. Only one person raced against Alexander Graham Bell, and his name was Elisha Gray. Gray came very close to winning one of the most important races in scientific history — the race to invent the telephone.

When Gray filed a caveat (which expresses the intent to file a patent later) describing a device "for transmitting vocal sounds telegraphically," he was only two hours behind Alexander Graham Bell. On the very same day, February 14, 1876, a friend of Bell's had filed Bell's telephone patent application. At the time, neither man had actually made a device that transmitted the human voice over electrical wire, but both believed they knew how. As events unfolded, however, Bell proved to be more determined than Gray; from February 14 to March 7, Bell — not Gray — worked feverishly to perfect the apparatus that became known as the telephone.

Since he didn't win the race, Gray is not as well known as Bell, but as a runner-up he certainly deserves honorable mention. Like Bell, Gray was an imaginative inventor, but unlike Bell, Gray's experiments stemmed from an interest in electricity rather than an interest in voice and sound. The son of a farmer from Ohio, Gray worked his way through Oberlin College, where he learned as much as he could about electricity. Like other inventors of the time, Gray was intrigued with the telegraph, and he worked hard to figure out ways to make it operate better. His efforts were rewarded with a patent in 1867, when he developed a relay device that improved telegraphic transmission of electricity. In 1869, Gray founded an electric-equipment company, which became known as the Western Electric Manufacturing Company when it relocated from Cleveland to Chicago.

While working at Western Electric, Gray turned his attention to the same problem that had fascinated Bell. "Was it possible," he wondered, "for the telegraph to transmit more than one message at a time?" Gray's efforts to find an answer were so much like Bell's you would have thought the two had shared a lab. Like Bell, Gray experimented with tuning forks and reeds, discovering that, at least in theory, several tones could be sent over one wire at a time. And, just as Bell had, Gray then reasoned that a great many tones, as many as can be produced by the human voice, could also be transmitted over an electrical wire.

As his caveat application showed, Gray did develop the plans for a transmitter that would send the human voice over electrical wire, but once he discovered that Bell had filed a patent, Gray simply gave up. Gray never did build the transmitter to see if it would work. Although Gray later made legal challenges to Bell's patent, claiming that the device described in his caveat was closer to a working telephone than the one that Bell had described, the courts eventually ruled against his claim.

In 1881, the Bell Telephone Company bought a controlling interest in Gray's Western Electric Manufacturing Company. By manufacturing Bell telephones and equipment, Western Electric became one of the world's largest and most profitable companies. By 1881, however, Gray had left the company to take a teaching and researching position at Oberlin College. In the race against Alexander Graham Bell, Gray came in second, a score that didn't count nearly as much as first.

The Telephone Show Hits the Road

Now that Bell and Watson had come up with a telephone that actually worked, they believed it was time to turn it into a commercial success. The two began to show other scientists as well as influential leaders in the political and business worlds just what the telephone could do.

The demonstrations were such a success that Watson, Bell, and his financial backers decided to form the Bell Telephone Company to manufacture and market the telephone. Founded on July 9, 1877, the company attracted many investors and was soon able to sell shares.

As the Bell Telephone Company grew, so did the use of the telephone throughout the United States and the rest of the world. The telephone rapidly turned into a huge communication system that presented a host of technical challenges. Fortunately, most of these challenges were met by creative and inventive people who worked to put Bell's invention within the reach of people all over the world.

Bell demonstrates the telephone in Boston in 1877, the year he formed the Bell Telephone Company. He sold most of his shares between 1879 and 1883, and the sales made him a millionaire.

— Chapter 2 —
The Telephone Becomes a Tool

It's a good idea to keep a pen by the phone, but in 1877, when Bell Telephone began, it was an even better idea to have a small hammer nearby. Since the very first telephones didn't have bells, the caller had to tap the phone to summon the person at the other end of the line.

But that's not all the caller had to do. Although the rectangular, box-shaped phones were small and easy to lift, it was still complicated to use the hole in the front of the phone that was designed for both speaking and listening. Callers had to bring the telephone box next to their mouths and speak loudly and directly into the hole to convey a clear message. Then, they had to quickly transfer the box and press it tightly against their ear to hear a response. Making a telephone call in 1877 required both patience and coordination.

Telephone Improvements Attract Customers

Because the first telephones were awkward devices, by the fall of 1877, only six hundred Boston residents had telephones. But many more people decided to give them a try after a few changes made telephones easy to use. In late 1877, Thomas A. Watson (Alexander Graham Bell's assistant) designed a crank-activated bell that gave the telephone a ring; callers could put their hammers away! And within a few years, telephones with separate ear pieces (or receivers) made telephone calling less of an acrobatic chore.

> **AMAZING FACTS**
>
> The first exchange was installed on January 28, 1878, in New Haven, Connecticut, and within months, switchboards sprang up all along the East Coast. Instead of stretching between callers, telephone lines went from the customer's home or office to a central switchboard center, where operators switched the lines.

But the improvement that attracted hordes of new customers was the switchboard, or the exchange, a system that enabled all the customers within one area to converse. Before exchanges, callers could only talk to a handful of people with whom they shared a direct telephone line. After the switchboard was invented in 1878, callers could connect to twenty or thirty other lines.

The switchboard was a panel of electrical control switches that received all outgoing calls in an area. When a call came to the switchboard, an operator would connect it through the appropriate switch with the telephone being called.

Many of the young men who worked the first switchboards responded to incoming calls only when they felt like it. (Apparently the operators were busy with chair racing, wrestling, and other indoor sports.) So, the Bell Telephone Company decided to employ women operators to replace the young men. The women worked out so well that Bell stopped hiring male operators for many years.

Another important improvement in 1878 was the invention by Francis Blake of a telephone transmitter that used carbon, which greatly improved the sound quality of the call. The modern telephone of today is remarkably similar to this telephone.

Here's how it works: When you speak into the phone, the air waves that carry your voice vibrate a steel diaphragm that's built right into the phone. The diaphragm presses against small particles of carbon whose electrical resistance varies depending on the pressure from the diaphragm. This process then makes vibrations in an electric current, which are exactly the same as the vibrations in

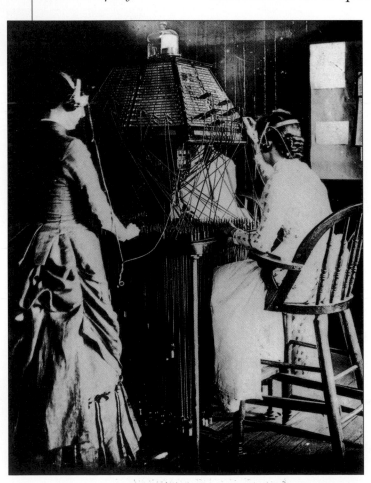

One of the earliest switchboards was the "Lampshade Switchboard" of 1882. The introduction of the telephone exchange greatly expanded the network of contacts for each telephone user, and phone use increased rapidly.

your voice. The electrical current then travels by electrical wire to a receiver, or the ear piece in the listener's telephone. In the receiver, the electric current travels through an electromagnet, which pulls against a steel diaphragm. The diaphragm vibrates and reproduces the sound of your voice.

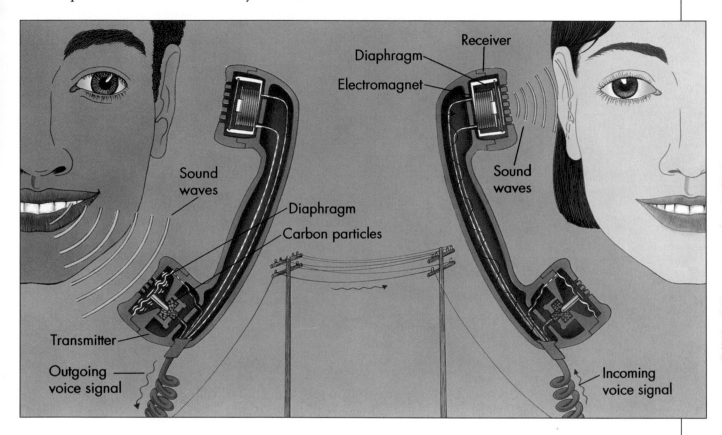

"Ma Bell" Corners the Market

Bell Telephone split into two companies in 1878: the New England Telephone Company, and a new Bell Telephone Company headquartered in New York City. Both companies issued licenses to smaller companies, keeping ownership and control. As the parent company that controlled all the "Baby Bells," this company structure also eventually earned Bell Telephone its nickname, "Ma Bell." By 1881, about 132,700 Bell telephones had been installed in homes and businesses throughout much of the country.

Telephone transmitters translate the sound of the human voice into electrical currents, and receivers turn these currents back into sounds a listener can understand.

Granville T. Woods (1856–1910)

As the Bell Telephone Company built its telephone business, it bought patented inventions from people whose work allowed Bell to maintain a competitive edge. One person whose work was especially important was Granville T. Woods, nicknamed the nation's "black Edison" because of his electrical genius. After Woods received a patent for a telephone transmitter that was superior to Alexander Graham Bell's, the Bell Telephone Company quickly bought it, knowing it could be used to improve telephone communication. But this invention was only the first for the creative Woods, who went on to receive more than sixty patents for electrical and other inventions that greatly improved communication and transportation systems.

Woods was born in Australia but immigrated as a boy with his family to Missouri, where he found a job in a railroad equipment shop. Locomotive engines fascinated Woods, and although his paycheck was small, he managed to set aside enough of it to afford lessons from a master mechanic. Soon, the Iron Mountain Railroad Company hired him as a locomotive engineer. But Woods was enterprising, and he wanted to work on his own. In early 1884, he and his brother used their pooled savings to begin an exciting new venture, the Woods Electric Company, which made telephone, telegraphic, and other electrical equipment.

Although the production work kept Woods busy, he still made time to experiment and invent, and within a few months, he had secured the transmitter patent that Bell Telephone bought. Only a few months later, Woods patented a second invention, which allowed operators to send either Morse code or voice messages over the same wire. Woods called the process telegraphony, and again, Bell Telephone recognized its commercial potential and bought Woods's patent.

While his work advanced communication, Granville Woods's contributions had important benefits for the railroads as well. Train transportation became a lot safer thanks to his work. In 1887, he invented a telegraph system that allowed moving trains to send telegraph messages to each other. Since the trains always knew the whereabouts of other trains, there was less chance of collision. After moving to New York City in 1890, Woods received patents for a series of inventions that improved the electric streetcar systems. A streetcar wheel he designed was called a troller, the source of the name for the trolley car.

Although Woods was once called the greatest electrician in the world, his talents and skills did not, unfortunately, lead to much fortune. Woods lacked the money to manufacture and market his inventions, and, in the late 1800s, almost all of the people who could have backed him financially were white. Despite Woods's obvious genius, racism prevented wealthy whites from supporting the work of an African-American. Nonetheless, his contributions to telecommunications and transportation are now recognized as important stepping stones on the path to the information age in which we now live.

The company's first two patents came from Alexander Graham Bell. After that, Bell Telephone bought other inventors' patents to expand its ability to make telephones and provide service. In return for a share of the profits, Bell Telephone issued a license to anyone who wanted to use the company's patents. Bell Telephone also chose to rent rather than sell telephones to its customers, an arrangement that ensured revenues for years to come.

Since it was obvious to American investors and businessmen that ownership rather than a license would spell larger profits, a number of companies went into the telephone business. One of the largest, the Western Union Telegraph Company posed a significant threat to Bell Telephone.

As Bell Telephone defended its patent rights in court, Western Union lawyers argued that Elisha Gray (who then worked for

This lantern slide of the early 1900s shows a man using the office phone to call his sweetheart. The telephone found a place in the world of entertainment — in movies, plays, books, and songs — in the early years of the twentieth century.

Western Union) had been the real inventor of the telephone. They claimed that after Alexander Graham Bell saw Gray's telephone plans, which were filed with the U.S. Patent Office only hours after Bell had filed his, Bell went back and changed his own patent application. But when Western Union was unable to produce evidence to back up its claims, it looked like they would lose in court. So, Western Union gave up the fight, and, in 1879, it also gave up its telephone business — fifty-six thousand telephones in fifty-five cities — to Bell Telephone.

When Bell Telephone's two major patents expired in 1893 and 1894, nearly five thousand small telephone companies emerged to seek business in areas where Bell Telephone had not. An area where the need was great was rural America. To farm families, the phone was as welcome as steady rain after a long drought.

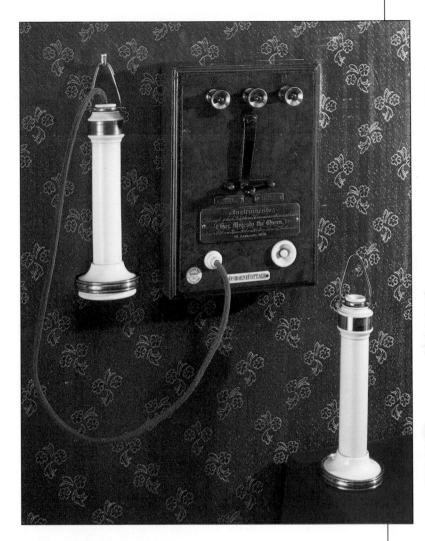

A Bell telephone used by Queen Victoria of Great Britain in 1878. Although telephones were in use in Europe by then, overseas telephone calls were not possible until 1926, when radio service was set up for that purpose. Even then, phone calls were often poorly transmitted when storms and static interfered with radio waves.

Relief and Emergency Help

In the early 1900s, America was overwhelmingly rural, but the farms that dotted the midwestern and western landscapes were few and far between. With its promise of instant communication, the phone provided relief from loneliness, emergency help, and even the morning and evening news! A few enterprising newsmen broadcast their reports from the local switchboard centers to anyone who cared to call in. For midmorning entertainment, some people would listen to their neighbors' conversations, as several families frequently shared what was called a party line.

Despite a few problems, such as gophers chewing through telephone lines, telephone use in rural areas increased dramatically in a very short time. From 1902 to 1907, the number of telephones in the rural areas of the United States increased or 450 percent.

For Every Problem, Inventors Found a Solution

Inventors were soon able to solve some of the early problems that first plagued telephone communication. One of the worst problems was static, and much of it came from the ground. To complete a circuit, the first telephone lines were connected by wire to the ground, which meant that the electrical energy beneath the earth's surface created disturbances along telephone lines. Described variously as bubbling, rasping, and gurgling sounds, these ground noises made it pretty tough to hear and be heard! But when two-wire circuits replaced the single wires (thereby eliminating the need for a grounding wire), they put an end to the concert of earthly noises.

As telephone use increased, the telephone poles between which wires were strung became higher and higher so that more crossbars could be added to carry more wire. On one street in New York City, ninety-foot poles with thirty crossbars held three hundred wires.

Wires and poles come down in a blizzard of 1888. In the earliest telephone systems, each call used a different wire. As the telephone gained popularity, higher and higher poles with ever more crossbars were installed.

When severe sleet and snowstorms made the heavy wires even heavier, they often collapsed, interrupting service for days. The problem was eventually solved when underground lead-covered cables were laid.

Telephones Reach Across Long Distances

Because it was a one-wire circuit rather than a two-wire circuit, the first long-distance line installed between Boston, Massachusetts, and Providence, Rhode Island, on January 12, 1881, was so full of static it could hardly have been termed a success. But soon the change to a two-wire circuit made long-distance communication clear, and Bell Telephone formed a separate division — American Telephone and Telegraph (AT&T) — to handle its expanding long-distance business.

One other problem remained: attenuation, or the tendency of an electrical impulse to weaken as it traveled long distances. From 1881 to 1884, attenuation limited long-distance calls to about fifty miles. But in 1884, it was discovered that taut copper wires caused less attenuation than the iron wires that were then in use. With copper wire, the calls stretched to about three hundred miles. But it wasn't until the invention of the loading coil in 1900 that attenuation was significantly reduced. Installed on intervals along telephone wire, the coils strengthened the electrical impulses, thereby strengthening the sound of the voice. Then, a device called a repeater was invented in 1913 that made sound waves traveling the telephone circuit sound louder than they had before.

On January 15, 1915, the first transcontinental phone call was made, from New York to San Francisco. The callers were none other than Alexander Graham Bell and his friend Thomas Watson. When Bell repeated his famous message, "Mr. Watson, come here, I want you," Watson replied, "It would take me a week to get there now!" Telephone technology had triumphed over incredible obstacles but the next few decades would bring even greater triumphs.

AMAZING FACTS

The first switchboard operators had to have excellent memories. Since there wasn't a place on the switchboard to write customers' names, the operators memorized which line belonged to which customer. But an epidemic of measles changed all that! As the disease spread through Lowell, Massachusetts, in 1880, the town doctor worried that if the operators became sick, no one would be able to operate the phones; they wouldn't know whose line was whose! He suggested that each customer be given a phone number that would match the numerical order of the incoming lines. The practice made the switchboards so much easier to operate that the number system was soon adopted by every exchange in the country.

— Chapter 3 —
A Communications Network Is Created

In the early 1900s, technological improvements helped the telephone grow from a local communication tool to one that was nationally shared. Improvements in transmission and switching technologies made calls clearer and reach farther than ever before. As the largest telephone company, Bell Telephone could provide lines that would interconnect with local independent lines. This gave many more customers access to long-distance calls, no matter which smaller company provided them with local service.

A busy Parisian telephone exchange in 1904. As the pool of connected users grew, the telephone became more important — and eventually essential — to the general public.

World War I Boosts Phone Service

World War I, fought from 1914 through 1918, created a strong demand for further expansion of communication systems in the United States and abroad. The United States entered the war in April of 1917, and its armed services immediately needed both telephone equipment and the lines and switchboard systems that would hook it all together. The United States commissioned the Bell System and independent telephone companies to help build a U.S. Army communications system in France. The U.S. Army Signal Corps in France built one hundred switchboards and over twenty-six hundred stations and strung one hundred thousand miles of wire to establish strong communication networks for the Allied armies defending France. Fourteen thousand AT&T employees joined the United States Army Signal Corps battalions, over half (seventy-five hundred) of whom were stationed overseas.

By this time, switchboard operation had been clearly established as "women's work." In keeping with the employment practices of the time, wages for the job were therefore lower than they would have been for men. Nonetheless, it was seen as a good occupation for women and seemed an excellent way to support the war effort to many. When General George Catlett Marshall, a distinguished American army officer, asked for female volunteers for a Women's Telephone Operating Unit in France, more than 7,500 women applied for the initial one hundred jobs offered. Eventually, 233 went overseas to operate the telephone systems, and some of these women worked under combat conditions.

Back at home, customer demand for telephone service continued to grow throughout the war. People needed to know of their loved ones in the conflict and to support each other, functions the phone helped fulfill admirably. Since the war effort increased orders for many goods and services made in the United States, the telephone's use as a business tool increased as well.

An American soldier in Europe in World War I. A huge U.S. Army communications system was set up in France once the United States entered the war in 1917. Massive amounts of telephone equipment were shipped to the French Allied command center.

A postcard of 1911 shows the telephone linking lovers. The phone was already popular with the public, but customer demand grew through World War I and the number of private telephone lines soared.

After World War I, this wartime increase in privately owned telephones changed the device from something that had been mainly a business tool and a luxury good to simply a common utility, like electricity or running water. Once the telephone had found a place in someone's home, the owner rarely chose to disconnect it. Once people had this new invention, they couldn't imagine living without it.

The Telephone Is a Hit

In fact, it became a standard prop on stage and found its bell ringing in books, movies, and popular songs. The telephone's failure to ring when wanted became a familiar theme, as in Irving Berlin's "All Alone":

> All alone, I'm so all alone,
> There is no one else but you.
> All alone by the telephone
> Waiting for a ring . . .

As a standard piece of equipment for daily life, the telephone began to find its way into the arts. Playwrights frequently used the telephone as the "fifth business," a stage term for a role acted

"What a time we'll have."

by a character who usually has no other function than to move the plot along. In Noel Coward's play *Sorry You've Been Troubled*, the telephone helps start the action, set up the plot, reveal the social connections and flaws of a main character, give a possible motive for murder, and even, although weakly, point to a suspect. Not bad for a small electrical device that was not even a member of the actors' union!

In another example of its stage presence, by 1928, the modest telephone was starring in a Broadway hit, *The Front Page*, which has been called "the ultimate telephone drama." The action of the play is shown through the device of an editor and reporters using seven telephones in the press room of the Criminal Courts Building in Chicago.

Telephones and the Great Depression

The Great Depression, which began with the U.S. stock market crash of 1929, was rather slow to hit the telephone industry. At first, the crash itself actually increased telephone business, as millions of calls were made between frantic stockholders and brokers. By the end of 1930, Bell Telephone subscriptions were at an all time high of 15,193,000 telephones in service, bringing the company earnings of $1.1 billion. Another reason for increased telephone calls and profits was that people needed to talk to one another about the changes the Depression was making in their lives; the economic disaster was at first a boon for the telephone industry.

However, after 1930, the number of telephones in use dropped quickly as people found they could no longer afford phone service. From 1930 to 1931, the number of telephones in service dropped by 292,000, the first decline ever. By the end of 1930, Western Electric (which was by then the manufacturing arm of American Telephone and Telegraph) had laid off 80 percent of its workforce, creating even more unemployment and poverty for the nation. No one was buying new telephones. In

AMAZING FACTS

The party line, which acts much like an extension phone in a home, was introduced in New York City in 1891, with two-party and four-party lines. But it was in rural areas where it really caught on. With the party line, a household could use the phone only if no other household on the line was using it. As with the home extension, one could pick up the phone to dial or hear the conversation of someone else on the line. This led to wonderful eavesdropping opportunities throughout rural America and anywhere else the party line invited people to pick up and listen for a dial tone . . . or their neighbors' personal business.

The newest fashion in phones in 1926. The boom in telephone use, begun in World War I, peaked in the late 1920s. Then, the Great Depression hit the industry. Many phones were disconnected, and thousands of telephone workers, both switchboard operators and those in manufacturing, were laid off.

fact, if they hadn't found some work converting telephones from manual to dial operation, the company might have had to lay off closer to 98 percent. From 1931 to 1932, the number of phones in service dropped another 1,650,000. Nationally, in 1932, one telephone in ten was disconnected. In 1933, long-distance calls were down to thirty million a year, compared to fifty million in 1930.

American Telephone and Telegraph decided there was no point in keeping workers on the job when the demand for phone service had fallen through the floor. Eighteen thousand employees — mostly switchboard operators — were laid off; the company simply had no work for them to do.

The workers who remained were asked by the telephone company to help increase subscription rates. Out of a sense of loyalty (and probably to hold onto their jobs), they often did more work for less money, or worse: In southern New England, where more than thirty thousand customers had dropped telephone service, the Southern New England Bell Telephone Company asked employees to work nights and weekends without pay, going door to door to find new customers.

Phones Make a Comeback

Gradual national and international recovery from the Depression returned phone use to where it had been before the stock market had crashed. Phone use then continued to increase as the economy got stronger.

Switchboards had improved to help keep up with demand, from the old panel switching, first installed in 1921, to crossbar switching, introduced in 1938. Both still required operators. Panel switching could connect up to five hundred terminals but was noisy and needed a lot of upkeep, while crossbar switching remained electromechanical, working more quickly and quietly. Crossbar switching could serve thirty thousand or more customers and made an important step toward what would become the computerized electronic switching system.

As the nation recovered from the Great Depression, American Telephone and Telegraph continued to build its monopoly on the phone business, owning 83 percent of all phones in 1939 with 16.9 million Bell telephones in service. At that time it owned 91 percent of the telephone manufacturing plants, 98 percent of the long-distance wires, and 100 percent of the transoceanic radio telephone systems. In 1939, toward the end of the Depression, American Telephone and Telegraph had a net company worth of five billion dollars, the largest amount of money ever controlled by a single private company. It could afford to support research that would lead to many exciting changes in communication technologies — and it had the money and power to squeeze out competition in almost any place in the United States.

This French magazine cover of 1927 foresaw the videophone, more than fifty years before it became a reality.

— Chapter 4 —
War and Prosperity Spur Communication

While the Great Depression had been poor in many ways for the telephone business, the Second World War was great for it. Just as World War I had increased the need for telephone communication, World War II boosted customer use because of calls between servicemen and their families, between business and government contractors, and between just plain folks needing to talk during this worldwide crisis. By the end of 1942, the number of long-distance calls had doubled compared to December 1941, when the United States entered the war in response to the Japanese attack on Pearl Harbor. But that was just the beginning.

Bell Laboratories in Murray Hill, New Jersey. The first buildings here were opened in 1941 to develop new communications systems in World War II. Most of the company's research activities since then have taken place here.

In 1942, three-quarters of a billion more phone calls were made than in any previous year. In fact, domestic business was so good that Bell Telephone begged customers to limit their phone use, asking "all civilians to refrain from calls to busy war centers, to limit all calls to five minutes, and to keep the lines as clear as possible from seven to ten P.M."

The company couldn't keep up with this demand in part because the armed services had created a stronger demand for equipment. Western Electric had turned into a major defense contractor, manufacturing communications and radar equipment instead of telephones for domestic use. At the same time, Bell Laboratories, the research and development arm of American Telephone and Telegraph, grew into a giant company in order to supply the Allied military with the new communications systems needed as the war raged from 1939 through 1945.

Peacetime Brings Prosperity

After the war, the demand not only stayed up, it increased! Changing back from a war economy to a consumer-driven one took a lot of communicating, but that was not the only reason telephones were in high demand. Servicemen and women returned home and joined all the other people who decided to start families now that the war was over. The population increased, creating more demand. Plus, the economy was growing richer; people could afford the new phones. By the end of 1946, Bell Telephone was installing new phones at the rate of twenty-five a minute on each working day.

Profits Pay for Research

The war effort had not only helped the telephone company grow, it helped pay for the research that led to new discoveries. In the process, Bell Labs became the greatest source of new inventions that the world had ever known.

Microwave radio, developed by Harold T. Friis, was one of the inventions it fostered. A closely guarded secret used in Europe and the Pacific during the war, microwave radio was further developed in peacetime into a system for transmitting long-distance calls by means of microwave relay towers. Microwaves are high-frequency electromagnetic waves that are in between infrared and short wave radio wavelengths on the electromagnetic spectrum. Microwave was first used experimentally in 1947 and went on to

AMAZING FACTS

In the 1940s, AT&T refused to put switches on their phones to turn them off and insisted that at least one phone in every home had to be able to ring at any time, day and night. Some customers objected to this invasion of their right to silence and privacy, but most were willing to suffer the consequences of being connected to others at the ring of a bell.

become the main carrier for long-distance telephones in the U.S. By 1975, Bell microwave radio would provide over 380 million miles (610 million kilometers) of long-distance telephone circuits.

When transmitting information, microwaves only need twenty watts of power to travel the twenty-five to thirty miles between towers across the country. Tens of thousands of microwave towers form a network across the United States. Microwave signals travel parallel to Earth's surface in a straight line, but they can be blocked by any obstacle, such as a tall building or mountain. They have to be supplemented by other telephone systems, such as underground cables and telephone lines.

A Tiny Invention Creates Huge Changes

Probably the greatest accomplishment of Bell Labs and the one tiny invention that, more than any other, created the world of communication as we know it was the invention of the transistor. This tiny device helped build the "information highway" that now leads us into the future.

The Bell Labs team of John Bardeen, Walter H. Brattain, and William Shockley discovered the transistor effect of semiconductors and then, in 1947, invented the transistor itself, for which they were awarded the Nobel Prize in 1956. The transistor has been called the key to modern electronics. Without it, we would not have communication satellites, space travel, or our quickly advancing computer industry, which is in the process of joining transistor-dependent telephones, modems, and CD-ROM to link up the world as never before.

Before World War II, researchers had been trying to replace the vacuum tube — used to amplify sound — with something less bulky, less fragile, and less heat producing. They started looking at *semiconductors*, substances through which electricity flows partially or imperfectly. Electricity flows freely through *conductor* materials such as copper, but through other substances, such as pure silicon, it hardly flows at all.

AMAZING FACTS

The transistor had many uses both in and out of the telephone industry. According to the *New York Times*, November 2, 1956, the transistor "created a boom in the manufacturing of hearing aids almost overnight because of the . . . size and low battery consumption" of transistorized hearing aids. So, from a technology that owed its start to Alexander Graham Bell's interest in hearing impairments and related fields, a debt of sorts was repaid to those whose hearing could be helped by transistorized hearing aids.

After the war, the Bell Labs team were able to continue their experiments with semiconductors. They found that when silicon is made impure — by adding phosphorous or germanium, for example — it conducts electricity partially, and this makes the electronic impulse stronger. This happens because the electricity builds up in the semiconducting material while it waits to pass through. This is called the transistor effect of semiconductors, because it both *trans*fers and is a re*sistor* of the flow of electricity. In telephones, amplification of the electronic impulse strengthens the sound of the voice.

Using the transistor effect of semiconductors, the Bell Labs team invented transistors by taking a pure crystal and cutting it into thin slices. Then, they heated the slices and exposed them to tiny impurities. After they attached wires to the layers, they put the finished transistor into a small protective case. They succeeded in making a tiny device the size of a pencil eraser that restricts, and so controls, the flow of electrical current in a way that amplifies or increases electrical impulses. Much smaller than vacuum tubes, transistors are difficult to damage, use very little power, and create very little heat.

The transistor invention led to the creation of integrated circuits in the 1960s. Some integrated circuits, such as the microprocessors used in computers, have more than a million transistors on a chip, as these circuits are often called. Transistors are commonly used in hearing aids, electronic equipment such as television and radio, communication satellites, and as electronic switching devices for phone calls, the use for which the Bell Labs team originally invented them.

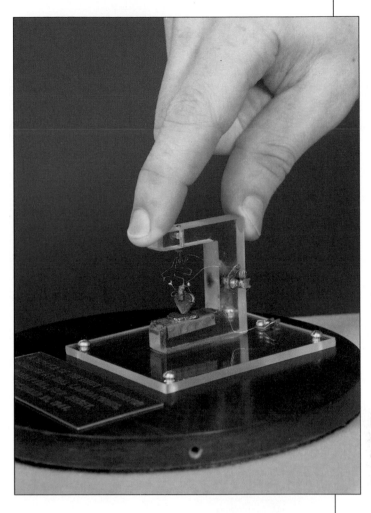

A replica of the first transistor, invented by a team at Bell Laboratories. The transistor gave rise to many new products, including Bell Laboratories' invention of the solar battery, which uses chemically pure silicon to which tiny amounts of impurities are added.

Walter Houser Brattain (1902–1987)

Although he was American, Brattain was born in Amoy, China, where his father, Ross R. Brattain, was a teacher at a private school for Chinese boys. However, Brattain's father and mother (Ottilie [Houser] Brattain) returned with Walter to the United States when he was still quite young. Brattain's father then became a cattle rancher and flour miller in the state of Washington.

The oldest in a family of five children, Walter Brattain attended public school in Tonasket before majoring in physics and mathematics at Whitman College in Walla Walla, Washington, where he earned a B.S. degree in 1924. He followed this by gaining his M.A. degree in physics from the University of Oregon in 1926 and, in 1929, he earned a Ph.D. in physics at the University of Minnesota. During the last year of his doctoral program, he worked for the United States National Bureau of Standards, improving the accuracy of time measurements and instruments that measure vibration frequency.

Brattain loved ranching and the outdoor life his father's homestead provided, but he hated farming. He later claimed that "following three horses and a harrow in the dust was what made a physicist out of me."

Hired by Bell Telephone Laboratories in 1929, Brattain's research on semiconductors was interrupted by World War II. From 1942 to 1945, both he and his Bell Laboratory colleague, Dr. William Shockley, were assigned to the division of war research at Columbia University, where they worked on magnetic detection of submarines and other scientific technology related to antisubmarine warfare.

After the war, Brattain returned to continue his work on semiconductors, which are solid crystalline materials that conduct electricity in unique ways. In 1947, Walter Brattain miniaturized electronics by applying the transistor effect of semiconductors to co-invent the transistor, a small electronic device with at least three electrical contacts and a semiconductor. A transistor is used in a circuit as an amplifier or a switch. Smaller, stronger and more energy-efficient, transistors replaced the larger vacuum tubes that had been in use in radios and other devices since 1902.

Brattain shared the Nobel Prize in 1956 with his colleagues, Dr. William Shockley and John Bardeen, for "investigations on semiconductors and the discovery of the transistor effect," which led directly to the invention of the transistor. When told he would get the Nobel Prize, Dr. Brattain modestly said, "Much of my good fortune comes from being in the right place, at the right time, and having the right sort of people to work with." The team split the prize money three ways. Their work is now applied to diodes (electronic devices that restrict the flow of electrical current chiefly to one direction), transistors, and computer memory devices of all kinds.

The Bell Laboratories team of William Shockley, left, Walter H. Brattain, and John Bardeen, right, in 1948.

Electronic switching systems make a number of phone features possible, from three-way conversations and conference calling to the automatic switching of incoming office calls over to a line that isn't busy. They also allow such common home phone features as call waiting, multiple line systems, and voice mail, which is a kind of answering machine-like feature provided by the local telephone company. Voice mail interacts with a number of features within a company's internal phone system or within the home customer's service, allowing call forwarding and responding to the message received.

International Calls by Cable and Satellites

In spite of all these improvements, direct long-distance dialing (phoning without going through an operator who would switch your call from wire to wire across the distance) was not available until 1951. Then, in 1956, transatlantic cable made international telephone calls possible. Unfortunately, these cables laid beneath the ocean were expensive to repair and weren't able to handle the large number of callers who wanted to speak to friends, relatives, and business associates abroad. A caller often had to ask the operator to make the call for them and then wait for hours for the operator to phone back and say the call was about to go through.

Researchers in the fifties began to look for more efficient ways to handle the demand for long-distance telecommunication services, especially for transoceanic phone service. They found it on August 12, 1960, when the first communication satellite, called *Echo I*, was launched. *Echo I* was simply an aluminized plastic balloon one hundred feet (thirty meters) in diameter. A passive satellite, it just acted as a mirror that received and reflected telephone signals. But, simple as it was, it was able to receive and reflect signals that had traveled thirty-five thousand miles (fifty-six thousand kilometers). Compared to the ordinary radio receiver that can only detect waves that traveled a maximum of one hundred miles (160 kilometers), this was a major improvement!

Signals were sent to *Echo I* by means of a huge, sixty-foot (eighteen-meter) dish antenna. The satellite was big enough to be seen by the naked eye and was able to transmit voices, wire photo pictures, and even television pictures, although these were somewhat fuzzy. All this was made possible by a Bell Laboratories' invention developed by Joseph G. Chaffee back in 1933. His supersensitive low-noise feedback FM receiver had cost more to run than other kinds of receivers, so it was never used . . . until *Echo I* needed it, almost thirty years later.

Echo I was followed by the launch of *Echo II* on January 25, 1964. This passive satellite stayed in orbit until May 1968, when it reentered the earth's atmosphere and disappeared.

Satellites Get Active

The next satellites, including *Telstar*, launched on July 10, 1962, were active instead of passive. This meant they could do more than just receive signals, as *Echo I* and *II* had done; they could amplify and transmit signals, as well. *Telstar*, which became the model for the communication satellites that followed, was developed by American Telephone and Telegraph. It was 34.5 inches (87.5 centimeters) in diameter, weighed 170 pounds (76.5 kilograms), and received signals from a huge, 380-ton (346 metric ton) antenna located on Space Hill in Andover, Maine. A slightly lighter active satellite called *Relay* was launched on December 14, 1962.

Active communications satellites work this way: An Earth-based transmitter first receives telephone, telegraph, radio, or television signals from sending stations. Then, the transmitter sends the signals

A model of Telstar, *the first satellite to both receive and transmit signals, designed by AT&T. Sensors onboard included solar cells to measure radiation damage and the angle to the Sun, and a Sun-reflecting mirror used in night sightings.*

over radio waves to the satellite. At this point, a device called a *transponder* amplifies the radio waves and then transmits them again, aiming them toward either another satellite or an Earth-based receiving station. Since there are no cloudy days in space, energy from the Sun (solar energy) is always available to power the transponder and other electronic equipment on communications satellites.

Syncom, launched in 1963, became the first satellite to have a geosynchronous orbit, which means that its motion in orbit keeps in step with Earth's daily rotation, so that it stays above the same point on Earth's surface, night and day. The *Early Bird*, launched two years later, is also a geosynchronous active satellite, but it is much larger than *Syncom* and has more channels.

Twenty-five Years of Change

After World War II, the simple black phone got a new rotary dial, but that was just the beginning. Style and color choices were introduced, and calls were connected faster. By the end of the sixties, people all over the world could make phone calls that traveled under the seas or flew through space as part of a complex communication network of cables, satellites, and microwave and radio towers. The telephone now connected country to country, ship to shore, space to Earth and back again, making the world seem smaller and faster paced than it had ever been before.

Syncom *was the first communications satellite to operate in a geosynchronous orbit. It was used in October 1963 to demonstrate transatlantic telephone communications with a phone call linking Geneva, Switzerland, and the United States.*

Chapter 5
The Telephone Reaches Out

In the early years of the telephone, no one was really sure how the invention could be used in daily life. A number of attempts were made to use the phone to provide daily news, sermons, wake-up calls, music broadcasts, and other experiments. Some of these uses are still available today.

The first groups of people to want telephone service were doctors, druggists, and especially businesspeople. They could all do business more efficiently with this kind of instant communication; it helped them make money and seemed worth the price.

In the beginning, the Bell Telephone Company was charging fairly high rates for its service, which discouraged most people from getting a home phone. As a result, in 1891, the New York and New Jersey Telephone Company served 7,322 business customers, but only 1,442 homes. The first telephone customers were those who could afford the new gadget and who saw an immediate, moneymaking use for the invention.

The Competitive Era Begins

However, Bell's two main patents expired in 1893 and 1894. This gave rise to about three thousand so-called independent companies, who competed with Bell Telephone by offering local phone service at cheaper rates. Before this, Bell Telephone had mainly served medium-sized to large cities — in fact, it refused to serve rural areas at all! But now the independents forced Bell

AMAZING FACTS

Like captains that go down with their ships, telephone operators were often the last in their towns to leave the scene of disaster, and many awards for heroism have gone to them over the years. When the Clearwater River in Idaho overflowed its banks and flooded a small town on May 22, 1948, Mrs. Allen, the local switchboard operator, received the warning call at 5 A.M. She quickly began to phone all the townspeople and warn them to leave their homes. By 7:30 A.M., flood waters were rushing down main street, so her son helped her lift the switchboard to a table to keep it dry. By 9:30, her office was in nearly three feet of water, but she kept calling until she was sure all were alerted. No lives were lost, and she received an award for her courage.

Telephone to lower its rates in order to keep its old customers. To still make a profit, Bell Telephone had to give service to smaller cities and towns as well. This gave the company a smaller profit, but from more people, so the money kept rolling in.

Bell Telephone refused to link independents to its national network of phone lines. Sometimes, independent companies would join together to give customers service to medium-distance calls, but they never equaled Bell Telephone's long-distance reach.

To fight for a piece of the business, some small companies introduced the party line as a cheaper way for customers to use the phone. Since a group of neighbors could share one line, it was cheaper to install and use than individual phone lines.

Farmers formed cooperatives to serve those rural needs Bell Telephone refused to provide. As more customers linked up with the system and as public pay phones became more available, telephone use became as familiar to people as the daily mail.

A woman using the telephone around 1890. Making a phone call took less effort than writing a letter and so quickly became popular. By the turn of the century, people were warned by etiquette books against occupying the line for long periods of time, being rude, and calling at inappropriate hours.

A Member of Polite Society

In fact, in many ways the phone call began to replace the letter as a way to communicate, and people gradually began to drop their old methods, such as visits, calling cards, letters, hand-delivered messages, and telegrams, in favor of the quick and easy phone call.

Etiquette books published between 1891 and 1955 showed a growing acceptance of the telephone for giving invitations to some events, although they warned that a verbal invitation was harder to refuse gracefully because you had to think up an excuse on the spot! In 1938, Margaret Fishback warned girls against bothering boys by telephone, while single men were told never to ask "Guess who this is?" By 1955, Emily Post devoted an entire chapter to correct telephone etiquette.

Women Rule the Phone Lines

Studies of telephone use in many western countries show that women talk on the telephone more than men do, probably because women tend to be the ones who organize social and family events. They also are usually given the job of providing emotional support to friends and family members more than men are.

This doesn't mean that men don't spend a lot of their time on the telephone, but that they tend to use the phone more for business and leave the social networking to women.

Social Interactions Change

With the telephone, social and business life began to move more quickly. Decisions that used to need a week or more for letter communication could often be made in a matter of a few minutes' conversation on the telephone.

A teenager today uses a mobile phone. Studies show that the women and teenage girls in a U.S. household will make more phone calls per year than will an equal number of men. Australian and French studies show that women make longer calls than men do. A study of the British shows that women call their relatives and friends more often than men call theirs.

It also made life less formal. While a person writing a business letter will take care to choose words and put the needed information in good order for the reader, the same person may call and then let the business information unwind in a casual, conversational style. With the telephone, people can change plans and quickly inform the others concerned, which helps make social activities less rigid and formal than the handwritten invitation and response approach had required. In addition, a sense of safety comes with knowing emergency help is available just by dialing 911 and other hotline numbers (suicide prevention, crisis intervention, teen hotlines, drug hotlines, etc.).

Erna Schneider Hoover

Erna Schneider Hoover began working at Bell Labs in 1954, where she developed and patented the first computer software used to switch telephone calls. She was one of the first people in the United States to get a patent in the software field.

Before her invention, telephone switches were controlled by hard-wired (or electromechanical) relay equipment, where connections are made by physical contact of selecting bars with holding bars, or by electromechanical switches operated by computers. Bell Labs had been planning to use computers for switching, but they couldn't find a solution to the problem of managing the large number of calls that the machine would face. They needed Dr. Hoover's invention to allow the machine to work no matter how many calls came in.

Dr. Hoover's solution attacked the problem from two sides. As she explained, "We needed a method to keep the computer from being overloaded when a very large number of persons tried to call at once, and my invention . . . involved measuring how busy the machine was and regulating the number of calls accepted as a result." Using her software, phone call traffic was smoothly directed so there were no "traffic jams" even at peak periods of phone use.

Dr. Hoover had attended high school during a time when, in her own words, "girls were supposed to act dumb even if they were not" and then attended Wellesley College, where she did honors work in medieval history and philosophy — not the usual course work for a future computer software inventor! She then went to Yale University to earn her Ph.D. in philosophy and the foundations of mathematics.

Dr. Hoover taught at Swarthmore College before she was asked to join Bell Laboratories' research teams, where she was one of the few women who had any real responsibility. Many women who had been hired in men's absence during World War II had been demoted to poorer jobs at the end of the war or left the company of their own accord. A wife and mother as well as a scientist, Hoover drew up the plans for her invention while she was still in the hospital following the birth of one of her three daughters.

The transistor technology needed for computerized switching was still so new when Hoover joined Bell Labs that it took the team years of hard work before they could operate the first electronic switching system in 1965. The final cost to develop the whole system was close to $500 million. When they were finished, the team had created a programmable digital computer to control the operation of a switching network. This was a tremendous leap forward in speed and efficiency — and a long way from the original circuit switching that connected calls by hand with cords and plugs.

Her invention and contributions to the Electronics Switching Project of Bell Laboratories allowed Dr. Hoover to become the first woman supervisor of a Bell Laboratories' technical department. She now advises women who want to work in male-dominated areas of employment to do their homework: Women should research the companies to which they apply and make sure that the company they work for has a good record not only of hiring women, but of training and promoting them.

Telephones Help Shape Architecture

Skyscrapers have been built since the phone became widespread. These New York City apartment-hotel buildings would not have been practical in the days when hotels employed messengers. By 1904, the Waldorf-Astoria hotel had 1,120 telephones involved in 500,000 calls a year. At the time, this was the largest concentration of telephones under one roof in the world.

Before telephones, hotels employed messengers who were called to rooms by a signal. Elevators and stairs were always crowded with messengers in those days. But by 1909, the hundred largest hotels in New York City had twenty-one thousand telephones — nearly as many, at that time, as did the continent of Africa.

Telephones allowed architects to design larger and larger buildings, so that skyscrapers are now a major feature of large cities. Imagine how many messengers it would take to carry business communications in a forty-story office tower!

The telephone also gives people a network of instant communication; now a person can go almost anywhere and be reached by telephone to conduct business. In fact, with the introduction of cellular phones, people's offices are often their cars, their backyards, in an airplane, or anywhere else they choose. The current trend toward home offices is made possible by such phones and by the telephone connections with computers, fax machines, and personal communicators that bring not only verbal but visual information from place to place in minutes.

Some folks don't want to miss any calls while talking on the phone and pay for call-waiting service or voice mail that will take a message while they're on the phone. On the other hand, some prefer the slower pace that comes with less instant communication, and many choose to vacation in places out of phone's reach. Others "let the machine get it," screening their calls through the answering machine. With modern telecommunications, there is a service style to fit almost any personality.

Chapter 6
The World of Telecommunications

With the use of fiber optics to send and receive telephone calls, modern telephones have returned full circle to one of Alexander Graham Bell's most promising inventions. In 1880, four years after he invented the telephone, Bell invented the photophone, which used a beam of sunlight traveling through thin air to carry sound from sender to receiver. In describing his favorite invention, Bell wrote to his father: "I have heard a ray of sun laugh and cough and sing!" However, on Earth, sunlight is only available during the day, and bad weather can block its rays. It wasn't until the 1960s and 1970s, when scientists invented lasers and optical fibers and then put the two together, that Bell's photophone could work in a practical way to carry phone calls.

Lasers work by producing light that is different than sunlight. The laser creates, amplifies, and then sends out a special kind of light called *coherent light*. Coherent light is made up of waves that are all the same wavelength and all in phase, or in step, with one another. Ordinary light is made up of many different wavelengths and phases. Laser light is very strong because, since all of its waves are the same length, they hit an object all at the same place and time. Today, lasers have very many uses in industry and in medicine.

When sent through optical fibers instead of thin air, laser light can carry sound (or other data, including visual data) at any time to any place the fiber can reach. An optical fiber is a very clear, flexible thread of glass, up to six miles long and thinner than your

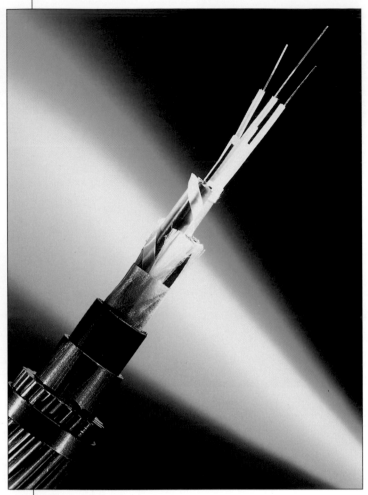

This cable is designed to carry conversations as pulsed, coded laser signals. The fiber optics filaments are seen at top right; the rest of the cable is shielding and protective layers. A light beam entering the end of the fiber is internally reflected from the cylindrical surface of the core so no light escapes.

eyelash. It is sometimes called a *lightguide* because laser light can travel through the length of the fiber and still stay bright.

The first optical fiber cables were installed in Chicago, Illinois, in 1977. They were threaded into the existing underground cable system, so they were relatively cheap to install. Fiber optic cables take up less space and weigh far less than copper wires, and they are not affected by storms or other sources of static because they transmit light instead of electricity. In 1988, American Telephone and Telegraph laid a fiber optic cable under the Atlantic Ocean between North America and Europe, followed by other optic cables linking communities throughout the world.

Close to the Speed of Light

The biggest advantages optical fibers have are speed and strength. Repeaters that correct for attenuation have to be installed every mile along copper wire cables, but only every six miles in fiber optics — even less often with new technology. Tests in June 1992 showed that a new system using wavelength division multiplexing and optical amplifiers can now boost the distance light-wave signals can travel from 43 to as far as 521 miles (69 to 523 kilometers). Wavelength division multiplexing (WDM) is a switching device that divides a single wavelength into several smaller channels to direct voice, data, and fax information simultaneously between each channel and destination. This system can carry up to six hundred thousand calls at once across the Pacific Ocean, its first planned use. Some optical fibers do not need repeaters (which amplify signals) because it was discovered in 1973 at Bell Labs that optical fibers to which the metal erbium is added actually amplify signals on their own — if the signals are sent at very high frequencies.

Most importantly, fiber optic cables are faster than copper wires. Electrical signals at higher frequencies travel faster in optical cables than in copper wires because copper has electrical properties called capacitance, inductance, and resistance that cause delays, attenuation, and power losses in the line. In addition, they can carry more than one set of electrical signals.

With active satellite systems and fiber optics in place, international telephone calls can be made by direct dialing without the help of an operator. Western European countries, such as Germany or the United Kingdom, have fully modern systems and connect easily with the United States. The United States and Japan are the best worldwide in terms of technology and availability to the public.

AT&T Plays to Win at Monopoly

In the old days, the near monopoly that AT&T (and its manufacturing arm, Western Electric) had on the United States helped to standardize communications because everyone was using the same equipment; in 1930, Western Electric sold 92 percent of all the telephones and telecommunications devices in the U.S. At the same time, AT&T served 80 percent of the local telephone customers across the country, so it controlled how the telephones were linked, both locally and nationally.

While the AT&T monopoly standardized the telephone industry, it also strangled the possibility of new ideas coming from other companies that want to do things differently. After a seven-year lawsuit brought by the Justice Department, the two sides reached a settlement in 1956, in which AT&T agreed to give the licenses on all its patents to any company, domestic or foreign. This allowed many other companies to enter the telephone market.

AMAZING FACTS

Push-button phones began in Baltimore back in 1941 but were too expensive to use until transistors helped bring the cost down. Touch-tone service was first available in 1963 and paved the way for many new uses of the telephone, including access to computers.

Alfred Y. Cho

Dr. Alfred Cho developed a process called molecular beam epitaxy, or MBE, which grows crystals used to make semiconductors. With MBE, crystal growth is controlled at the atomic level, so the crystals become extremely precise semiconductors. Most of the laser chips in compact discs are now made by his MBE process. Communication satellites also use semiconductors made with MBE crystals because they require so little amplification and are sensitive enough to detect signals that are very small, or very far away, as most satellite communication signals are.

Born in Beijing, China, Dr. Cho grew up in Hong Kong and then came, at age eighteen, to the United States to attend the University of Illinois. There he earned his B.S. degree in 1960, his M.S. in 1961, and his Ph.D. in electrical engineering in 1968. He also met his wife, Mona Willoughby, there, and they now have four children, all pursuing scientific or medical careers.

Dr. Cho joined Bell Laboratories in 1968, where he has been director of semiconductor research since 1990. He currently holds forty-six patents on crystal growth and semiconductor devices related to MBE. His process has led to many incredible inventions, including quantum cascade lasers which can produce different wavelengths of light and the discovery of unexpected electron transport properties moving in a semiconductor.

Scientists at Bell Laboratories are now using Dr. Cho's MBE method to lay down crystal film that is only a few atoms thick, called a quantum well. This film is thinner than the wavelength of an atom's electron, so the electron particle can only move in two dimensions, instead of the usual three dimensions we expect from physical reality.

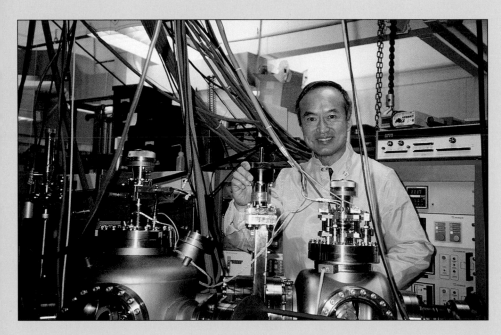

Alfred Cho with molecular beam epitaxy (MBE) apparatus.

Dr. Cho says that to invent, it helps to apply past experiences to new situations. When he took his experience in surface physics and ion propulsion, which he learned on another job, he was creative enough to use it to develop his new crystal growth technology, MBE. Through MBE, he was able to create, in his words, "an ordered growth of one crystalline layer upon another." His process allows the crystal to transmit electrical impulses at extremely high densities and speeds with very little noise. This is now used to make the world's fastest transistors.

When he was first working with MBE technology, some people told Cho, "Sorry, that . . . won't fit into our production schedule." He realized they didn't want to make any changes in the way they were doing things. He knew at that point that "it was very important for me to believe in myself, to persevere, and to have vision."

That vision led to his great discoveries and to high honors as well. President Bill Clinton awarded Dr. Cho the National Medal of Science in 1993, and the Franklin Institute awarded Dr. Cho the Elliott Cresson Medal in 1995 — the same award that had been given to Alexander Graham Bell, the inventor of the telephone, in 1912! Both men will long be remembered for their important contributions to telecommunications, and, in turn, to the world we live in today and the technology that will carry us into the future.

In spite of this, antitrust lawsuits continued to be filed against AT&T by other companies throughout the 1960s and 1970s. AT&T was forced to give up its Bell Operating Companies (BOCs), a big loss. They were formed into seven Regional Holding Companies.

AT&T Finds New Business

On the plus side for AT&T, it was then allowed to enter the computer and information business by creating AT&T Information Systems (first called American Bell). It created several new laboratories, staffed mostly by former employees of Bell Labs, and these labs have worked to bring fiber optics to the seven Regional Holding Companies. Other companies, such as Sprint and MCI, raised money to build fiber optic networks because this new technology would attract customers and help them compete with

Engineers attend to a junction box of fiber optics cables. These cables weigh far less than the copper wires used in both above- and below-ground telephone cables. A single spool of optical fiber can carry as many messages as two hundred reels of copper wire.

AT&T. Clearly, this new competition has helped to move the development of fiber optics forward.

The main research activities of the now-smaller Bell Labs continue to be fiber optics, computer software, and the microelectronics that increasingly shrink the space needed to perform computer and electronic tasks. Other companies with their own research divisions work both separately and, at times, in joint efforts to explore the amazing possibilities of telecommunications worldwide.

─── Chapter 7 ───
Highway to the Future

The Bell Telephone Laboratories now join with computer and other businesses and telephone systems worldwide in the effort to connect all of the world's communication systems into one integrated "information highway." On this highway, computers can "talk" to fax machines, mobile phones, televisions, and other computers, and telephone lines can do tricks, such as transfer photographs through modems to computer printouts.

From its earliest days, the telephone has made a huge difference in the ways people connect with one another and with the world of information. Today, as it links more kinds of information through fiber optics and other technology, it continues to change the way we live our lives and conduct our business.

Simple Codes for Complex Information

The key to building an information highway is finding ways to hook up information and communication machines worldwide so that all can send, receive, and also code and decode one another's "languages." Just as the telegraph, the first long-distance communicator, used electrical signals to represent language, today's information machines use two kinds of electrical signals to send all information, whether it is in the form of words, numbers, sounds, or images.

The two types of signals are *analog*, which means continuous, and *digital*, which is made up of just two levels — high and low. The digital signal is similar to the signal created by the telegraph's Morse code, which consists of two units — dots and

Computers, phones, and fax machines, as here, already allow many people to work at home. When all communication systems become compatible, even more business will take place away from offices. Travel patterns will change drastically as less people commute daily.

AMAZING FACTS

The Sony Corporation and AT&T PersonaLink Services joined together in 1994 to offer a personal communicator called Magic Link that receives and sends e-mail as well as fax, phone calls, or paging services. Slightly larger than a paperback book and weighing only 1.2 pounds (.5 kilograms), it is advertised as easier to pack on trips than a laptop computer.

dashes, or long and short electrical impulses. Part of the challenge of building the information highway is to allow machines using these two different electrical signals to talk to one another with understanding and also to quickly "translate" their signals into the sounds, numbers, images, and spoken and written words that people understand.

Some inventions, such as fax machines (which transfer facsimiles, or look-alike images of paper documents, over phone lines) have been around a long time but are now connecting to computers through on-line services and modems. Modems translate the analog signal, which most local phone lines still use, into the digital signal that computers use. Since digital signals have only two levels, high and low, any information (voice or video) can be represented by a set of digital signals or digital code. Information in digital form can be transmitted faster by reducing the number of digital bits required to send a given message. This is called data compression.

Other Connection Options

ISDN, or Integrated Services Digital Network, is a digital transmission service, first used in the late 1980s, that businesses can dial up as needed to connect desktop computers to voice, data, and images sent from other computers, telephones, fax machines, and other information devices — all at the same time over one pair of copper wires. It is cheaper and slower than ATM, or Asynchronous Transfer Mode, a higher grade version that competes with it. Both ISDN and ATM are much faster than a modem, but the various components of the systems are still made by a number of sources and don't always connect as well as users would like.

A GSTAR communications satellite is tested. These satellites, launched from 1984 to 1990, form a network with Spacenet satellites to provide domestic telecommunications, data transmission, and video-relay facilities across the globe for U.S.-based companies.

Practically an extension of the human being, the modern telephone comes in many shapes, sizes, and degrees of portability. Here, a transparent, perspex phone reveals the components inside.

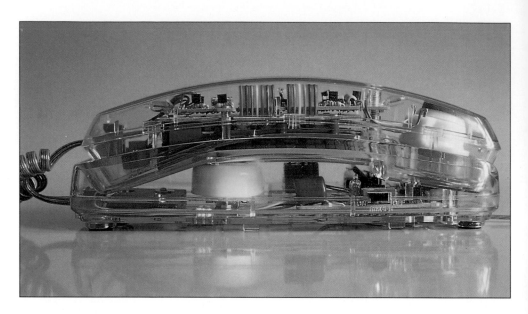

The information highway is still in its infancy but gradually coming of age as the local infrastructure, or the connecting web of fiber optics, cables, and radio and microwave relays, is woven together with the connection options we've just described.

A new vehicle on the information highway is the personal communicator, first marketed in the midnineties. This is a cellular phone and computer combined. Hand-held units, they are able to bring and send voice, fax, e-mail (which is electronic "mail" sent between computers through modems and phone lines), and paper messages while the user is away from the usual desktop machines. This is great if someone wants to take the office to the beach. But when will someone put the beach on a microchip so we can take it to the office?

Cable Connections, Then and Now

In the first telephone systems, a single wire was used, which limited how fast and how far the information could go between repeaters. This was improved by stringing two wires together to make a complete circuit for sending and receiving. Then, it was found that wire pairs worked better when they were twisted together. Modern telephone loops are usually made of this

AMAZING FACTS

Fiber optics have many uses outside of telephone communication. For example, optical fibers are bundled together and packed into a flexible, slim tube to make an endoscope, a kind of medical spyglass that doctors can slip into a patient to take a careful look inside the throat, lungs, intestines, or other parts of the body.

"twisted pair" cable threaded underground. But coaxial cable, which is two or more copper-based cables separated by insulation and enclosed in a flexible metal sheath, while originally designed to carry telephone services, now primarily carries cable television.

The success of fiber optics and microwave radio systems has slowed research on cable systems at this time, but, like other ideas that must wait for the right moment, it could find other uses in the future. In the meantime, coaxial cable allows telephone companies like Ameritech to offer a "video dial tone network," which provides regular cable TV along with two-way interactive services that range from personal banking to ordering groceries.

Don't Leave Home Without One

The days of the "Star Trek" communicator that is just a tiny device pinned to one's chest may not be fantasy much longer. We are already able to use a phone without any cords attached, and microelectronics keeps making our machines smaller and lighter.

An example of this freedom from connecting cords is the cellular phone, first demonstrated in 1979. The cellular phone uses radio waves sent from tower to tower in a honeycomb system across the country. Cordless home phones use the same radio waves to connect the much shorter distance to the base phone, which then sends and receives calls through the home's own installed conventional wires or fiber optics.

With the right connections, telephones can sometimes act like a human being all on their own. For example, some companies program their telephones to mechanically dial numbers and offer recorded-voice sales choices to their customers. When

A woman uses a cellular phone from her car. Towers that receive and transmit radio waves are situated right across the country. As people travel by car or plane from cell to cell in this system, their phone connection passes from tower to tower as they move.

such a sales pitch meets with an answering machine, we see robot social life in action: One machine is talking to another; no human being is directly involved.

Many commercial institutions often program their answering machines to offer many options to people calling from touch-tone phones. A person calling a bank's information number will be told, "If you'd like to know your account balance, press one, NOW. If you'd like to know your last three deposits, press two, NOW," and so on, through many numbered choices. Some American college students can select their courses and schedule in a matter of minutes just by pushing the right numbers on a touch-tone phone. Their parents used to spend a day or more in long lines to achieve the same results!

A Wireless World

The future looks increasingly cord-free as companies compete with one another for the mobile market. For example, Mtel and Microsoft are working together to combine pagers with computers to make a Nationwide Wireless Network. It will start in three hundred cities, working off receiving stations so the two-way communicators don't need antennas and can last a month on batteries. The hand-held communicators can send voice or hand-written messages to computers or connect with phones, fax, computers, or e-mail. Compared to this, regular mail will seem more like what e-mail users already like to call it — "snail mail."

Companies are finding that wireless technology costs much less than building an in-ground cable system, and the future of television may very well be a system based on a cellular phone network, such as the one CellularVision of New York has been testing. It will serve cable TV programming over the air to receiving antennas within a three-mile radius.

The future that technology promises will be one in which everyone's hand-held computers can communicate with one another without wires or cords, from anywhere to anywhere, any

AMAZING FACTS

Competition for a share of the broadcast spectrum is fierce. There is a limited amount of space on the spectrum, and in the United States, the government regulates who can send and receive on the airwaves and assigns them a spot on the bandwidth. In this system, cellular telephone and paging companies must bid against television broadcasters for their licenses in multibillion-dollar open auctions.

time. These computers may well respond to voice commands and be able to read your handwriting . . . and send your scrawled note in an e-mail birthday card to your sister in Hawaii alongside a video image of you as you make her a cake. You'll be able to sing "Happy Birthday" to her as you watch her read your card, and with the push of a key, she'll be able to smell the chocolate. In fact, she'll be able to interact with you in every way except to take the cake. That will not — even in the foreseeable future of the information age — be compressed and sent from tower to tower or bounced off a satellite.

Into the Information Age

The telephone has had a major effect on society both in the country in which it was invented and worldwide. It has helped bring people closer together and added to our sense that we are all, everywhere on the planet, just a phone call away. This little machine has saved lives, sent information around the globe, united friends and family, and yet, at times, stubbornly refused to ring or interrupted us more than we like. As we have seen, it has helped shape the way our cities are built and allowed people to conduct business out of their homes and cars.

The telephone is a strong presence in the heart of almost every home, business, and public institution. New uses for it continue to be found as changing technology finds more ways to connect it to us and our machines.

A woman speaking into a videophone can see the image of the person she is talking to. Cameras above the videoscreens of both users record their images and transmit them to the screens.

Timeline

1837 — Samuel F. B. Morse invents the telegraph.

1876 — Alexander Graham Bell applies for a patent on his ideas for a telephone.

1877 — Bell forms the Bell Telephone Company to manufacture and market the telephone. Thomas A. Watson designs a crank-activated bell that gives the telephone a ring.

1878 — The switchboard is invented at the same time by both Alexander Graham Bell and William Gray. Francis Blake improves sound quality with a transmitter that uses carbon.

1881 — The first long-distance line is installed between Boston, Massachusetts, and Providence, Rhode Island.

1892 — The first Strowger step-by-step automatic switching system is installed.

1913 — The invention of the "repeater" makes sound waves on the telephone circuit sound louder than before.

1915 — The first transcontinental phone call is made, from New York to San Francisco, from Alexander Graham Bell to Thomas Watson.

1947 — Microwave is first used experimentally to transmit long-distance calls. The facsimile (fax) machine is invented. Walter H. Brattain, William Shockley, and John Bardeen invent the transistor.

1956 — The first trans-Atlantic cable is laid under the ocean.

1960 — *Echo I*, the world's first communication satellite, is launched.

1962 — The first active satellites are launched, including *Telstar* and *Relay*.

1963 — Touch-tone service is introduced. *Syncom*, the first satellite to have a synchronous orbit, is launched.

1965 — The first computerized electronic switching office is installed in New Jersey. The Trimline phone is introduced.

1977 — The first optical fiber cables are installed in Chicago, Illinois.

1988 — American Telephone and Telegraph lays a fiber optic cable under the Atlantic Ocean between North America and Europe.

1994 — Sony Corporation and AT&T PersonaLink Services join to offer a personal communicator called Magic Link that receives and sends e-mail, fax, phone calls, and paging services.

Further Reading

Asimov, Isaac. *How Did We Find Out About Lasers.* New York: Walker and Company, 1989.

Asimov, Isaac. *How Did We Find Out About Microwaves.* New York: Walker and Company, 1989.

Billings, Charlene W. *Fiber Optics, Bright New Way to Communicate.* New York: G. P. Putnam's Sons, 1986.

Englebardt, Stanley L. *Miracle Chip, the Microelectronic Revolution.* New York: Lathrop, Lee & Shepard Books, 1979.

Giscard d'Estaing, Valerie-Anne. *The World Almanac Book of Inventions.* New York: World Almanac Publications, 1985.

Herda, D. H. *Communication Satellites.* New York: Franklin Watts, 1988.

Kohn, Bernice. *Communications Satellites: Message Centers in Space.* New York: Four Winds Press, 1975.

Laspina, Agnes F. *A Telephone and a Team.* Philadelphia: Dorrance & Company, 1973.

Lodewijk, T. et al. *The Way Things Work.* New York: Simon and Schuster, 1973.

Lukashok, Alvin. *Communication Satellites: How They Work.* New York: G .P. Putnam's Sons, 1967.

Math, Irwi. *Morse, Marconi, and You.* New York: Scribner, 1979.

Quiri, Patricia Ryon. *Alexander Graham Bell.* New York: Franklin Watts, 1991.

Schefter, James L. *Telecommunications Careers.* New York: Franklin Watts, 1988.

Skurzynski, Gloria. *Get the Message: Telecommunications in Your High-Tech World.* New York: Bradbury Press, 1993.

St. George, Judith. *Dear Dr. Bell . . . Your Friend, Helen Keller.* New York: Putnam & Sons, 1992.

Webb, Marcus. *Telephones: Words over Wires, The Encyclopedia of Discovery and Invention.* San Diego: Lucent Books, Inc., 1992.

Glossary

Analog transmission: Sending a continuous jumble of frequencies in which data is represented by variable physical quantities, such as sound frequencies from very low to very high notes.

Angstrom: Unit of length equal to one hundred-millionth (10^{-8}) of a centimeter.

Atom: The basic unit of an element. An atom consists of a dense, positively charged nucleus surrounded by a system of electrons.

Binary code: A code using only two numbers (*0* and *1*) to represent data.

Crystal: A solid structure with natural plane sides formed by a repeated pattern of atoms, ions, or molecules that have fixed distances between them.

Digital transmission: Sending data as a stream of pulses representing *0* and *1* (binary code), or *on* and *off,* or *positive* and *negative.*

E-mail: Electronic mail that comes over a phone line through a modem to a computer.

Epitaxy: The growth of the crystals of one mineral on the crystal face of another mineral in such a way that the underlying layers of both minerals are facing the same direction.

Infrastructure: The basic supports that make up a system, such as cables, satellites, telephones, and modems for the telephone system.

Micron: Unit of length equal to one millionth (10^{-6}) of a meter.

Modem: A device used to connect computers through phone lines to one another and to other machines, such as fax machines.

Molecular beam epitaxy (MBE): A way to grow crystals in a vacuum so that their atomic structure is precisely controlled.

Optical amplifiers: Spliced segments of optical fiber containing erbium, a rare earth element, used to amplify light signals sent through fiber optics.

Semiconductor: Crystalline material that conducts electricity more than insulators but less than good conductors.

Transistor: An electronic device containing a semiconductor that amplifies and controls electric current, used in a circuit as an amplifier or a switch.

Wavelength division multiplexing (WDM): Transmits light pulses over various wavelengths of light.

Index

Numbers in *italic* indicate pictures; numbers in **bold** indicate biographies